The Empress

Gayatri Lakhiani Chawla

Hawakal Publishers

Published by Hawakal Publishers, 185 Kali Temple Road,
Nimta, Kolkata 700049

Email: info@hawakal.com

Website: www.hawakal.com

First edition (India): May, 2018

Cover designed by Chitrangi

ISBN: 978-93-87883-10-9 (Paperback)

Price: INR 165
US Dollar 6.99

To my mother, *Sunanda*

ACKNOWLEDGEMENTS

Humble gratitude to the editors for publishing my poems in their print and online literary journals: "12 Gulmohar Road" was first published in *Narrow Road* (Aug 2017), "Hiraeth" was first published in *The Bombay Review* (Dec 2017), "L'amour" and "Felling" were first published in *The Anthology of Modpo poets* by University of Pennsylvania, "De-coding" was first published in *The Hans India*, "In Anticipation of Amber" was first published in *The Criterion* (Oct 2017) and "Arms and the Woman" first appeared in *WE Scream* by Rhythm Divine Poets. A lot of these poems were written during the Global Poetry Month with *The Missing Slate*—a platform dedicated to writing poetry during the National Poetry month, April. I am thankful to poet friends who read and encouraged my writing, Vinita Agrawal, Nabina Das, Jhilmil Breckenridge, Amit Shankar Saha and Smeetha Bhoumik. Special thanks to Linda Ashok for awarding me the second prize for the National Poetry Contest 2018 organized by Ræd Leaf Foundation for Poetry & Allied Arts. Loads of thanks to Kiriti Sengupta for his patience and encouragement. Much thanks to Hawakal Publishers for giving a home to my collection of poems.

All work of art is done in unison, hence, I thank Tarun and Uditi for believing in me and always being around. I'm grateful to Lakhiani and Chawla families for their undying love and support. Sonali, thank you for listening to me everyday, and loads of love to Vivek for his unbiased review of my work. Lastly, my gratitude to all my friends who appreciate poetry and support me.

CONTENTS

BITS OF A WORKING RESTAURANT

She comes from a small quaint town of Amasya,
to work in a fancy diners in Istanbul
she wears a red polka dotted scarf everyday
as part of her attire,
elbow deep in soapy water of a sink
she cleans piles and piles of dirty plates
her eyes are romantically locked at the cleaner boy from
Greece.
He lives in a small apartment
sharing it with eight other people.
He dreams of marrying the Diner owner's daughter
She is nineteen and sophisticated,
his kind of girl.
His eyes look like those of a caged animal
He is craving for freedom
He misses home and the warmth of his mother
On days like that,
He unbottles all his somatic energies into mopping the
floors.
The floors sparkle like the pieces of broken glass
scattered by the waiter a refugee from Aleppo.
Every time the manager yells at him
He can hear him crystal clear
unlike during the airstrikes back home.
He wishes never to go back,
He prays the roof above him doesn't blow off
He is grateful for the food on his plate.
Next weekend,
She will wear more make up

hoping the cleaner boy takes notice,
the cleaner boy will accidently
 brush shoulders with the Diner's daughter,
the waiter will embrace the truth
that this is Home and he is safe.

INTERPRETATION

How do you interpret small miracles in the Universe?
the *palash* all in bloom, looking ruby red like a *devi*
 from a distance,
a baby's cry so shriek
capable of waking the dead in the dense forest,
the cantaloupe opening like a vagina
with countless sunshine seeds of hope,
the burning of a pink candle
on new moon luring new love,
blowing the fluffy nucleus
of a dandelion upon a wish,
a mother rocking her adopted child
teary with the astounding news
of an angel in her womb.
'What is the source of all this'? asks the seeker
the child who is only eighteen moons old
stands up from the tribe sitting in a circle,
"I think the Sun is the reason of our being
the metaphysical prologue to life"
Silence prevails as truth

           c

               a

          s

               c

         a

                d

                  e

                    s

from the mouth of a child,
"and what is epilogue?"

asks the curious seeker.
"Again the Sun that sets every day,

the beginning of the end
the end of the beginning"
the affable child proclaims,
his eyes are closed, semi ennobled, he looks like a
messiah.

MILIEU

1

Handpicked tea leaves
from the tea estates of Darjeeling
two teaspoons of green tea
in flame a story on its own
the story of an earnest tea gatherer
behind that light –colored tea
infusing a pinch more than
taste, flavor and aroma
in my cup of green tea.

A sip of tea transports me
to the lush green hills of Darjeeling
I see a silhouette, a mother of two expecting her third
wearing a floral traditional dress.
Early spring she plucks the tea leaves ardently,
putting handful of tea leaves
into the carrier basket tied to her back,
her back aches with the heaviness of debts
inside there is a storm that is brewing,
outside she smiles at the tourists taking her pictures
Click, Click, Click…

2

Last summer at a tea leaf reading session
the fortune teller with bad teeth grinned
while she peeked into my teacup
looking for a pattern or symbol
What was that? I wondered
A tree, a human, a flower.
Next summer I was blessed with a child,
I suitably called her
Iris
Messenger of the Gods
The Goddess of the rainbow.

BONDAGE

Arranged marriage is like buying a crate of mangoes
They stare at your body from head to toe

        Touching the soft supple skin of the
mango
They look at your dark complexion, disappointed
           Shoving the green
mangoes away for the sunshine yellow ones
They look at your breasts, a sign of fertility
       Inspecting which ones are bigger and
juicier
They gauge your height, your weight, the size of your
vagina
       Holding the mango erect and
examining it visually
and then
      How much?

BODY

Who does my body belong to?
I should think it belongs to me
Unlike my eccentric lover
who wants to possess it,
He says 'you are mine'
like I am a piece of land or a herd of goats
that graze the Alpine pastures of Kashmir.

The night after the hurricane
often my body shivers feels like a refugee
crouching in the bushes with a kukri in my hand
guarded and armed,
awareness creeps into my skin
when a pair of eyes look at my unrobed flesh
piercing through and through,
at that moment I hate
I hate with my gut-wrenching mouth that curses the
evil,
Come sunset I will forget everything
and tame my mind to cut off that feeling.

Sometimes my body is a bric-a-brac of fallopian tubes
moving ahead like a traveler with a florescent lantern
the womb, a cocoon
safe, nurturing for the next life,
never believed I would give birth
to another tiny body,
until I held her,
how she slept in the warm comfort of my body
did she know she was her own body now,

do they ever.

My body belongs to me and me alone,
Just like
the soft velvety peach belong to my mouth,
the magenta nail varnish belongs to my toe nails,
the sweet words of love to my ears,
the dark enchanting kohl to my wide eyes.
Look at me if you please but mind the gap
lest I swing my double-edged sword.

ARMS AND THE WOMAN

He thinks she doesn't know of his animality
How he pilfers, a lump of clay in the dark
from the garden outside her house.
Every year tip –toed, head covered
his hands move like a raccoon
digging the auspicious clay.
On a full moon day
The air smells of the fresh rainwater
the night is a gypsy dancing queen
melting in the arms of her lovers.

She adorns her golden anklets, her neckpieces
her coiled hair braided neatly to one side,
lips smeared with a honey balm.

She wears her underwings of grace
standing majestically , a mace in one hand
Devi

RAIN
[Based on a Sindhi folk tale of Sasui and Punhoon]

From the shadows of the mirage
she appears like a ghost
Oh! Sasui is that you,
Is that you my love
come to me Sasui like the first rain
like the teardrops that drench my restless soul
quench the parched sandy terrains of Bambore
I know not of another
like you my beloved.
The clouds are a shade of noir
Punhoon takes shelter under a banyan tree
suddenly a flash of lightening
two feet away a sparkling fountain of truth.
Water, the substance of life
transparent, aqua , pure
flowing towards his naked feet
Punhoon peers to see his reflection
only to find his lissome Sasui.
The truth frees you
Much like the rain

GAYATRI

My mother is lionhearted like the warrior
who heads a one woman army,
she listens to her heart and her heart alone
holding the hand of a stranger
from the lands unknown.
My father is zealous like the Sun
that radiates the Earth and infinite skies
giving a meaning to our lives everyday.
My lover is my alter ego
always sitting next to me,
my home is the dark corner of my balcony
where I bask in the twilight, the in betweens
neither black nor white maybe grey.
I am a mystic river that flows
through the Himalayan mountain ranges.
I am daughter of the Sun God
Violet
Valiant
Victorious
is my second name.
I begin as a tiny grain of sand, a foreign body
I end as a rare pearl in an oyster, absorbed.

FOLKTALES

A golden ring with a lion's head etched on it
a wife caught in the waves of hazard
'Revive a little, I'm daughter of the wise sage
Vishvamitra
the birthplace of virtuosity
the creator of the Gayatri *mantra*
at least look for yourself
in the eyes of your child,
memory is a genetic disorder.
Slice me not like an apple my love,
but like the moon that sits
outside your window sill
every night nibble a little wedge from the corners
savouring is key
as said to *Hiraman*, the talking parrot.
Come escape with me across the bridge of darkness
O pretty one
I claw the deer skin's hide to entice you
satan is a sorcerer.
Apostrophe is a moment of reflection
before stealing someone's land
                    someone's woman
                    someone's dream.
Period is the yarn of time
and also a full stop.

JOURNEY

Across the limitless horizon of golden sunshine
my heart is a bird today,
it flies, it flies
to a country unknown to me
my soul deep like the muddy rivers that flow
it hums, it hums
to the beat of the glistening rain
my hands weary, mud-crack like
touch the leaves of the tree of life
they sing, they sing
the enchanted tale of the blue skinned God
my feet sway for the journey home
they dance, they dance
naked in abandon.

IRIS

Last night you drank from the goblet of love
intoxicated in the abyss of self
many moon years back
a two -feathered creature
banished from the Seven Kingdoms
descends to seek the Divine,
a barren queen wishes upon a new moon
engulfed in her tears
as the Water God emerges
'Unearth the truth' says he
It's a prophecy
With the break of dawn
history is etched
a new ruler is born, 'Iris'

BLOODY MARY

Like the rock salt that corrodes the tiny steel spoon
in the yellow ceramic jar,
a flicker of tubelight in my kitchen
is a presence of a passing spirit.
The arrival of the dark beady eyed raven
flying down from the *peepal* tree
his eyes fixed on a piece of meat
I carve on the kitchen sill.
Amavasya night my waist length hair get all knotted up
I want to pick up a pair of scissors
Snip Snip Snip
At the entrance of the house
Kolhapuri *chappals* left in haste
Resting titled one above the other,
a symbol of travel
my dead aunt used to say.
Strange noises from the apartment above mine
strange because it's 1 am
and yes, it's vacant.
I didn't see my alter ego
becoming a demon from hell
whispering "Jump right in"
as I stared at the Niagara Falls
looking seductive and wicked.
Signs of mental illness
Depression, a feeling of withdrawal
being delusional.
I sit to peel and cut beetroot
I gape
I have blood on my hands

the color of a vampire
blood is flowing from my hands onto the floor
Just then there is a doorbell
What now!

12 GULMOHAR CROSS ROAD

When I go back to my growing up years
I see my home fragmented
into small spaces and even smaller corners.
The house that I called my abode
amidst the lush magenta bougainvilleas
looked ever so small when I visited it last year,
the walls that I scribbled on
wore a dull blue tone like a shipwreck
a cloud of absence loomed over it now,
Was there a presence? Perhaps the ghosts of my
ancestors
One can always sense these things,
the rooms were dressed with dust-covered bed sheets
and I inhaled a thousand street noises from the east
facing balcony,
conversations flew to me like fragile winged butterflies
bringing a chest of memories and a guest called
melancholy.

And as I struggled to shore
I keep the kettle to boil,
learning the secret of life
everything comes back to you.

HIRAETH

That summer we left our childhood behind
in the darkling mango orchard,
before we knew it
 the julienne carrots and turnips
left to sour and pickle
in the scorching sun,
before we knew it
grasping the stone-fruit in our fists
as if the sky had fallen
the lightening felling our wrists
leaving our *chappals* in the yard,
the porch lights switched on
awaiting our quiet return
we walked away,
before we knew it.

SHELLS

Am I unlovable?
I ask
You say nothing
pretend not to listen,
you love me less and less
a little less than yesterday.
Do we outgrow each other?
             the *sindoor*
                  the *shankha*
                    the *pola*
the blowing of the egg-white conch,
that night as I smiled
at my *aalta*-dyed shy feet,
seems like from another pilgrimage.
Cognition
because I am used to standing
with you along the vast shore
the waves lapping at our tired feet,
we sit a little apart
the grainy sands sketching thumbnails of us.
Our destinies are blindfolded
much like our tastes in each other,
we are clogged by the pastel white
circlets of conch shells that adorn my wrists.
Poetry ebbs like an avalanche,
Ruin is a gift.

CURSED

"Do you believe in past life regression?"
The words were crystal clear
resonating with the brass cowbell sounds
that hung outside my east facing window.
The tarot lady had gingerly pulled out
a two of cups,
a battery of attractions and emotional connections.
I know I had read somewhere
there are no coincidences only encounters,
so was meeting him in the elevator real
and the power failure out, a hallucination
a ten minute enclosure
with a stranger
who looked like the person
I loved
but
lost
to
death.
It was a little eerie
felt like a time warp
I tried to say something
but my mouth was dry
I was brain dead.
I was catching a fever with the tension
building between us,
Suddenly the elevator starts working,
He steps out
I stay back till I get to my floor
Only to stare at the lobby lights
that were gleaming all through the day.

TAROT READINGS

There are days when she pretends not to see me
acknowledge my presence
believe in my existence
such remorse hatred
just because I am the devil
the devil in her deck of favorites.
When I come to her in a reading
silence is quite for a while
Air, Water, Fire, Earth
Elements of my desire
I do what I want
I do what I please.
Are you scared too?
I am innocent like that,
I remember one time
I got pulled up for
'What does the Universe have for you?'
Agony, violence, temptation
I am three in one
packaged in glittering gilded wrapping paper
with a crimson bow at the top
What swag!
But can't the devil have a heart
So I promise decorum
soon I will become a thing of the past,
as you shuffle away with a twinkle in your eye.

I CALL YOU BY MY NAME

Spinning the time wheel
I spin a yarn
a tale of two mirroring souls
memories are like fireflies
they light up your heart
align your body, your soul
to the first encounter.
We stood on the same rope bridge
staring, then suddenly
walk towards each other
how our shadows melted
in the lyric aubade of a blue night
awakening of a another kind.
If kissing was a man
I would ask him to sit beside me
Don't leave my side
Alas! I cling your arm,
stands of wavy hair,
long floral skirt
shards of emptiness
memorabilia mostly
brooding mostly

I call you by my name
'Athena Athena'
You stop, stare and move on.

JE NE SAIS QUOI

How very strange the one habit I abhorred about you was the very image that stayed with me in time- the smell of Gold Flake cigarette on a rainy day, the wetness of the earth and tobacco was intoxicatingly combustible. I was at a *mushaira* night at a friend's place the scent of rose flowers infused fragrance and poetry. Outside, the clouds had started their own *mushaira*, it was the first monsoon shower, rain drizzled softly, the leaves of the money plant creepers swayed in the breeze as I took in the smell of wet earth along with a waft of Gold Flake. You were standing close by near the balcony jean clad *kurta* kind, disheveled, you looked lost or heartbroken or both. With the dim Chinese paper lanterns bobbling above our heads, I smelled your cigarette smoke much before I saw you. Am I as missed as you? I thought. I never confessed how I wore your full sleeve white shirt one entire day to just be in your skin. It smelled of you and holding hands and walking in the rain. Do you remember the wetness of that day that's seeped into our bodies, our souls, our lives forever?

In a room with walls of a dozen people no words were exchanged, only eyes locked in the backdrop of the heavy Mumbai rains.

L'AMOUR

That year in that delirious spring
love letters were exchanged
without a word mumbled or said
volumes and volumes were spoken.

A small telegraph office
became the raison d'être for him
the reason to be
the reason to survive,
the intensity of their blaze poisoned his being
as he wrote letters like a lunatic
in the palm oil lamps.

What is love after all?
Words in envelopes made of linen paper with golden
vignettes
Stealing an hour from a day to pour a glass of passion
into paper
His mother shouting, "You are going to wear out your
brains"
"No woman is worth all that"
Still more writing, more letters, more frenetic
correspondence.

The letter unfolds and in between the words lies a
camellia,
the flower of promises is what he sent her
She was young, unsure hence she returned it
Only to receive another letter this one being the last
It was the year they fell into devastating love
Love in the time of Cholera.

MUMBAI

from the twelfth storey perceive an island of deities
in the humidity an incense of joie de vivre

inhale the spirit of Mumbai

THE YEARNING FOR HOME

That time of the year again,
when you, grandmother, stand
outside, hunching a little to the right
the plum beetroots bleed into
a tapestry of second skin
as I scoop a teaspoon of pickled turnips
preserved, cobwebbed spices
remains of a land called Home.

FLIGHT 1947

Rubber slippers forgotten in haste
walking bare feet
naked realization
dawned upon an *amavasya* night.

Jamshed Quarters stands tall and stoic
the lights have been switched off
I look away a sea of fragments
ahead, an oyster of tear drops

Notes:
Amavasya — No moon night.
1947, the year of the Partition of India, is symbolic of
displacement and isolation. It was a moment of emotional
turmoil as overnight our family left their homeland, Sindh,
forever. *Jamshed Quarters* was our ancestral home in Karachi,
Pakistan.

DE-CODING

For an hour I wish to go
to the land of the dead
to sit with the departed souls
and breathe the same air.
Close your eyes, I am told
to inhale their virtual existence and meditate
Why do all journeys end here?
are their vast skies bluer
do their bougainvillea creepers bloom early
do their wedge of geese
flock more align
more symmetrical than ours
do their widows blink their glass eyes
at the pregnant monsoon clouds
more often than ours
do their children never return from school
do thousands of their books, schoolbags and shoes
vegetate in the lost and found lockers
in this land of the dead is there a God
maybe
a Messiah
maybe
a spineless soul
maybe not.

FELLING

Manoeuvre from the tangles
of the poppy fields
that wrap around you
like sea-weed
criss-crossing in between
your hands, your legs
swaying a childhood dream.
Your mouth is the opening of a cave
A cloud of bats circling as if possessed,
your tongue
a sea urchin guarding a burning secret,
your fingers knitting the clock backwards.
The ink runs dry on the paper scroll
untouched
like the dinner laid out on the table

Suddenly, I'm dying

QUATRAIN

Sleeping nails under rip van wrinkled sands
loneliness hovering the brick wall poster
please leave the corridor lights on
Bloody life is such a stir

FLYWAY

Refugee camps dusting the roads
under dim lamps stories are woven

train journeys from distant lands
arrivals, departs moments stolen

words whisper in a contaminated voice
a storm raging inside their bellies.

What does it mean to be alive?
alive and breathing
Where do I belong?
Is this home and is it safe?

Across the field the cries are loud
could be the wild wolves on the prowl

a little boy is selling drinking water
terrifying eyes reflect cyclonic waves

the lady with the strange yellow balloon pants
is picking up her laundry

folding the white linen
placing it in a wicker basket

they look like the creases
on her broad forehead.

A coterie of old men are sitting
around a patient bonfire
fire-flies take refuge in the evening dusk

ENGLISH SUMMER

My body aches with the pain
the soul parched in your absence
the red swing rests stillborn
not a leaf has moved since.
Dear Robin, you must miss him too
awaiting the pieces of cheese on the garden table
I wish he would miss me a little
Maybe I'm not indispensible at the moment
love seems a stupid word
unpredictable like the English weather
but it is this that I miss my love
so come back home
like the first monsoon shower,
wet wild whispers
on the white patio.
I'm holding an umbrella
standing outside Kew Gardens
trying to remember
our first encounter.
What was it that struck me
a waft of wet earth
or your fresh breath
holding hands in a tight clasp
we promised till death do us part
I'm sorry I broke our promise
Fate was fighting with time
on that stormy night
Years have passed since

I'm waiting